Stegosaurus Up Close

Plated Dinosaur

Peter
Dodson, PhD

Illustrated by Bob Walters
and Laura Fields

Zoom
In on
Dinosaurs!

CONTENTS

Words to Know

dinosaurs (DY nuh sorz)—Reptiles that lived from about 230 million years ago to 65 million years ago. They had a special kind of hip and long legs.

fossil (FAH sul)—Parts of living things from long ago. They are often turned to stone.

mammal (MA muhl)—An animal that can grow fur and make milk for its young.

pterosaurs (TAIR uh sorz)—Reptiles that flew. They were not dinosaurs, but they were relatives of dinosaurs.

reptile (REP tyl)—Animals with scales that live on land and lay eggs. Dinosaurs, turtles, crocodiles, snakes, and lizards are reptiles.

Pronunciation Guide

Allosaurus [AL uh SOR us]

Ceratosaurus [suh RAT uh SOR us]

Diplodocus [dih PLAH duh kus]

Kentrosaurus [KEN truh SOR us]

Lexovisaurus [lek SOH vih SOR us]

Ornitholestes [or NITH oh LES teez]

Stegosaurus [STEH guh SOR us]

Tuojiangosaurus [TOO oh jee ANG uh SOR us]

A Plated Dinosaur

Stegosaurus was a strange-looking **dinosaur**.
It had plates along its back.
It had spikes at the end of its tail.
It was about as long as a school bus.

Head and Teeth

Stegosaurus's head was long and low.

It had a beak at the tip of its jaw.

Its mouth had almost 100 small teeth.

Its brain was tiny.
Stegosaurus was not very smart!

Body and Plates

Stegosaurus had a humped back.

Tall, kite-shaped plates of bone ran down its back.

The plates of *Stegosaurus* formed a double row.

The tip of the tallest plate was twelve feet off the ground!

A *Stegosaurus* plate is a piece of bony armor that is wide and flat.

Legs and Feet

The back legs were long and straight.

The front legs were much shorter.

Stegosaurus was probably one of the slowest dinosaurs.

Allosaurus

Tail and Spikes

Stegosaurus had four long spikes at the end of its tail.

It swung its tail to fight off enemies.

Big hungry meat eaters, such as *Allosaurus*, were very dangerous. *Ceratosaurus* was another enemy.

They may have eaten young *Stegosaurus*.

Food

Stegosaurus held its head only three feet above the ground.

It ate low plants like ferns, mosses, and bushes.

Perhaps it reached taller plants by standing on its back legs.

Babies

Just like all dinosaurs, *Stegosaurus* hatched from eggs.

Scientists have not yet found **fossils** of its eggs or babies.

In 2007, they found footprints of a baby *Stegosaurus*.

Its footprints were the size of a quarter.

Babies may have had very small plates or none at all. For now we can only guess.

Home

When *Stegosaurus* lived, the world was much warmer than it is today.

Stegosaurus lived on dry ground. There was a large, shallow sea near its home.

Ferns and other plants grew.

Stegosaurus Was Not Alone

Diplodocus

Stegosaurus lived with long-necked dinosaurs like *Diplodocus*. There were also two-legged plant eaters and armored dinosaurs. They all tried to avoid meat eaters, such as *Allosaurus* and small *Ornitholestes*. Fish, turtles, and crocodiles lived in the water. Tiny **mammals** lived on land. **Pterosaurs** flew in the sky.

Allosaurus

Ornitholestes

FOSSILS FOUND:

● = Stegosaurus

= Kentrosaurus

= Lexovisaurus

= Tuojinangosaurus

Many *Stegosaurus* fossils have been found. They show scientists that *Stegosaurus* lived in Colorado, Utah, and Wyoming.

Just as you may look like people in your family, *Stegosaurus* looked like its relatives, too! They all had small heads, plates on their back, and spikes on their tail. *Kentrosaurus* lived in Africa. *Lexovisaurus* lived in Europe. *Tuojiangosaurus* lived in China.

Learn More

Books

Dixon, Dougal. *Amazing Dinosaurs.* Honesdale, Penn.: Boyds Mill Press, Inc., 2007.

Holtz, Thomas H., Jr. *Dinosaurs: The Most Complete, Up-to-Date Encyclopedia for Dinosaur Lovers of All Ages.* New York: Random House, 2007.

Stewart, Melissa. *My First Time for Learning Dinosaurs.* New York: Publications International, Ltd., 2007.

Web Sites

Enchanted Learning. *Zoom Dinosaurs.* http://www.enchantedlearning.com/subjects/dinosaurs/

The Natural History Museum. *Dino Directory.* http://kidsdinos.com/

INDEX

For Julia Violet

Bailey Books, an imprint of Enslow Publishers, Inc.

Copyright © 2011 by Peter Dodson

Library of Congress Cataloging-in-Publication Data

Dodson, Peter.
    Stegosaurus up close : plated dinosaur / Peter Dodson.
        p. cm. — (Zoom in on dinosaurs!)
    Summary: "Gives young readers an up-close look at Stegosaurus
        and how its features helped it live"—Provided by publisher.
    Includes bibliographical references and index.
    ISBN 978-0-7660-3334-4
    1. Stegosaurus—Juvenile literature. I. Title.
    QE862.O65.D643 2011
    567.915'3—dc22   2009012286

Printed in the United States of America

052010 Lake Book Manufacturing, Inc., Melrose Park, IL

10 9 8 7 6 5 4 3 2 1

Illustration Credits: © Bob Walters and Laura Fields

Cover Illustration: © Bob Walters and Laura Fields

To Our Readers: We have done our best to make sure all Internet Addresses in this book were active and appropriate when we went to press. However, the author and the publisher have no control over and assume no liability for the material available on those Internet sites or on other Web sites they may link to. Any comments or suggestions can be sent by e-mail to comments@enslow.com or to the address on the back cover.

♻ Enslow Publishers, Inc., is committed to printing our books on recycled paper. The paper in every book contains 10% to 30% post-consumer waste (PCW). The cover board on the outside of each book contains 100% PCW. Our goal is to do our part to help young people and the environment too!

Note to Parents and Teachers: The *Zoom In on Dinosaurs!* series supports the National Science Education Standards for K–4 science. The Words to Know section introduces subject-specific vocabulary words, including pronunciation and definitions. Early readers may need help with these new words.

Allan A. De Fina, PhD
Series Literacy Consultant
Dean, College of Education
Professor of Literacy Education
New Jersey City University
Past President of the New Jersey Reading Association

Philip J. Currie, PhD
Series Science Consultant
Professor of Dinosaur Paleobiology
University of Alberta
Edmonton, Alberta
Canada

Bailey Books
an imprint of
Enslow Publishers, Inc.
40 Industrial Road
Box 398
Berkeley Heights, NJ 07922
USA
http://www.enslow.com